Challenge Your Comfort Zones

Slap yourself in the face with a fish

Well, did that catch your attention?

I hope this chapter will encourage you to look again at how you do the everyday, routine things linked to classroom teaching. We all want to feel energised and challenged when we deliver lessons, rather than a bit like a mouse on a treadmill. You can make a massive difference to your working life if you reappraise how you go about the basics.

Now: you can either buy a fish, or read on and think about moving your desk…

Classroom environment

Creative teaching starts way before your students ever set foot in your classroom. You need to ask yourself some uncomfortable questions and take brave chances with the way you interact with your teaching space.

As a first step try to look at your classroom from the perspective of a student:

- Is the environment warm and welcoming or is it cold and sterile?
- Does it have a personal feel to it, or is it just another classroom?

Try to make your classroom uniquely different, and then work to share ownership of the space with the students.

Classroom environment

Setting up the room

Look to set up a room that engages the students as an extension of their learning experience, rather than as a place where learning is enacted on them.

- Make your classroom as interactive as possible. This will challenge and stimulate the students and enhance the status of your subject. A resource table of reference books or subject magazines is ideal

- Curiosities are stimuli – plants, fish tanks, junk shop curios and other oddities can work for you. A colleague has a witch's broomstick mounted on his wall, something which fascinates and engages the students

- Aim to set your room up to create an atmosphere of working with the students – ask them how they'd like the room set up

Make your room distinctive. This helps make your learning environment interesting and engaging.

Classroom environment

Using the space

The way you interact with your own teaching space is crucial: right-handed people tend to favour that side of the room, and left-handed the other. Students recognise this and so if you are right-handed you'll find:

- Attention-seekers will be on that side of the room
- Quiet students will be at the front on your left-hand side (your real blind spot)
- The genuinely disgruntled will place themselves towards the back on the left. (Over a run of early lessons, you unwittingly ignored them when they offered to contribute)

Run this scenario in your head – the chances are you will either have trouble remembering who sits in your blind spot area or you will realise that they are the 'invisible' students you can't quite put a face to.

Classroom environment

Using the space

You need to counteract your preferred-hand bias, so instil a dynamic atmosphere by careful coverage of the room.

- Make yourself move and talk to each student at least once in every lesson
- Drill yourself to talk and teach from at least three different parts of the room each lesson

This approach helps develop a participatory atmosphere as students know that you will be accessing them all at some point of the lesson.

Classroom environment

Where can you put your desk?

The position of your desk sets the territorial rules for the room. Do you set up a block of teacher territory under the board, buttressed with filing cabinets to one side of a desk in front of the board? I call this the 'Somme set-up' – all you need is a machine gun on your desk and you have the perfect them and us statement. It shouldn't come as a surprise if students set up zones of their own on their side of the room.

Classroom environment

Where can you put your desk?

Put your desk where the students would least expect it.

At the wall opposite the board is a good spot. This will create two 'fronts' to your room – ideal for a range of activities as you develop a good working relationship with your students. It also means that you will have to move around the room rather than anchoring yourself to one spot. In this way you avoid teacher 'blind spots', those desks that are never visited and students who never engage with whole-class activities.

Classroom environment

Display's the thing

You can use display as a very easy way of generating group work as well as giving a sense of self-esteem to your students – especially as it allows students to select and evaluate their own materials.

- Try to encourage a mixture of student displays, bought displays, positive messages, key words/advice, and plants
- Aim to block areas of colour using sugar paper, or paint if you can win over the head of department – look to put blocks of displays or colour breaks at roughly eye level in the room

By allowing your students to personalise their learning space, and encouraging them to feel part of the learning process, you will boost their self-esteem and put them in a good frame of mind to engage with tasks that you set.

Classroom environment

Display's the thing

You can stimulate student interest and curiosity by the unexpected use of display work.

- Look for interesting/unusual areas for display, eg below the board, on your desk, on students' desks, or on the ceiling
- Mix displays from different year groups together. This can also be used to show how work progresses through the school
- Teach using display work as the core stimulus. For example, a maths lesson on co-ordinates could use displays as fixed reference points

Look to make display integral to the learning experience rather than just decoration. Don't be afraid to invite students to move and interact with display to understand work – 3D modelling on computers for ICT or in maths is enhanced if students have a real 3D model to look at and touch. Likewise, abstract equations and ideas can be reinforced by a permanent display that students can see every time they are in the room.

Classroom environment

Sharing key information

To support creative learning, it is good to work
with the students to create a room that engenders a
positive atmosphere. Mobiles and largely irrelevant
hangings can be fun, but don't miss the opportunity to
reinforce key ideas by pegging them up on 'washing lines'.

- Peg maths or science equations across the room
- If you teach a practical subject like design technology, hang old tools on
  the walls as conversation pieces. Students can then link them to their modern
  equivalents
- 3D models of shapes, planets and stars help students 'see' abstracts
- Pictures of famous people linked to the subject can be mounted on cardboard and
  hung from the ceiling. This will also give value to your subject

You can then ask students to use the mobiles in their work, or simply as
points of stimulus.

Three principles for creative planning

There are three guiding principles for you to consider when setting up a run of work:

1. ***The student should be at the centre of the learning process***, helping to shape it, not standing outside the process and having it poured over them like a bucket of water.
2. ***Help the students to develop skills*** they can use and develop independently of the teacher, *and in other subjects*.
3. ***A lesson needs to be viewed as part of a narrative.*** A sense of story helps creatively connect learning and aids reinforcement and memory.

How you can set up a sense of narrative

It's a good idea to simplify schemes of work so students can readily understand them. They can then be issued to students and displayed on classroom walls.

As parts of the scheme of work are being covered, they can helpfully be identified using highlighting pens, in effect encouraging students to move through the scheme as in a story.

This gives students a context for learning and associated activities. It also creates a sense of working together, which is crucial for student development.

Share marking criteria

Similarly, assessment criteria and simplified National Curriculum levels should be shared and displayed in the classroom. Discussing this information with students helps them to see how assessment works. It leads, in the long term, to students being able to produce their own assessments and marking criteria.

- Aim to involve the students in making displays that give key information – it will help them remember and give them ownership of ideas
- Take key advice from exam board documents and make this into a display
- Take short elements of the literacy strategy and ask students to create a wall of advice. For example, use displays of connectives as a focus for writing frames. Students must use three or four of the words from the display in their work

Use display to foster teamwork and independence for students in your classes, as well as a way of deepening their understanding of assessment processes.

Key questions to ask yourself

A major challenge is to stop seeing yourself as a teacher of 'subject x', but to move towards seeing yourself as a teacher. These questions should begin to challenge your fundamental assumptions about delivery:

- Why am I standing here? Where you stand dictates how you deliver the lesson and engage with the students. If you stand at the front you tend to talk a lot, but don't move and engage with the students

- Why am I talking? Telling your students is not as half as effective as them finding out for themselves. Verbal tasks simply need to be written on to the board for reference, freeing you to move around the room supporting students as they work

Key questions to ask yourself

Use the following questions to sharpen up your delivery:

- What do I want the students to get out of the lesson? (This allows for a tight focus and leads to better and more creative planning)

- Is there a brisker way of covering this work?

- Am I engaging all learners with this? Imagine delivering the same lesson content to a class made up entirely of visual learners, then kinaesthetic learners, then auditory learners. This will let you plan effectively for all learning styles

- Why would students want to come back to my lesson?

Key trigger for creative outcomes

Imagine having to teach where there is an absolute ban on any written outcome. Try feeding this idea into your own teaching and see where it takes you and the students.

Where are you now?

Wanting to develop creative teaching approaches links to a definite series of steps. See where you are – if you bought this book, go to at least step two immediately!

5 I am keeping the ideas that worked, and developing others of my own.

4 I have tried some ideas and some worked.

3 I am worried that the ideas might not work *for my students*.

2 I have got some ideas, and am thinking of how to use them.

1 I would like to teach more creatively, but need ideas.

As you move through steps 1-3, and out of your comfort zone, your personal anxiety will increase, but as you reach steps 4-5, you will feel more confident. Over a period of two or three years you will then build another comfort zone, and will need to revert to step one!

Starting Out

Setting the tone of a lesson

It is essential to engage the students the moment they arrive, and to move quickly into a task. This will give a sense of purpose to the lesson. Don't faff about with the register – take that once the lesson tasks are underway.

- Greet the students at the door to the room. Try to remember something about each student to use next time you meet – for example a success outside of your subject involving sport, or a birthday
- Involve students by using them to distribute textbooks and other lesson materials
- Praise whole class for work done last lesson, then punctuate the lesson with individual praise as you circle the room

The first five minutes of the lesson set the tone for what follows. Use them to your advantage.

Shocking!

Once in a while it might be good to really challenge the students with the unexpected. The element of surprise is effective if used sparingly.

- Hire a costume! Teach a maths lesson dressed as a superhero
- Sit on a desk on a chair with a box on your head pretending to be a medieval knight on horseback. (These two are great fun, but be sure to warn colleagues who are likely to pass the room what is happening!)

Shocking!

- Remove all the chairs
- Hide the lesson instructions; students have to find them
- Teach the lesson outside
- Change the desk layout within the room
- Criticise the actor/actress/band that is currently flavour of the month with the students. This will certainly get your class to engage with you
- Start the lesson with a joke or riddle

Two simple starter activities

You can use these to quickly engage all students with the lesson content:

1. Use pictures. Typically, get students to say or write down four or five things from a picture given to them upon entry to the room. This can be developed in the lesson by adding a selection of other pictures, and inviting the students to assemble their own textbook page using the pictures plus any text of their own they wish to include.

2. Write questions on pieces of paper. Give them to students randomly upon entry to the room. This becomes the student's/group's line of enquiry for the lesson. At the end of lesson students outline their line of enquiry and what they have found out. Alternatively, pick a few students to read out their questions for the whole class to work on.

If you give this kind of material out at the door, students have work to get down to straight away, so these are useful starters to settle a class.

Using text and key instructions

You can adapt the main text to be used in a lesson very effectively as a starter. Rather than just reading through information, try the following:

1. Matching work – write information on paper, cut in half, distribute randomly. Students have to find the other half of the information. For example, match characters to events in English and History, or object to word in MFL, or unite two halves of an equation for Maths and Science. Similarly, you could write questions and matching answers on separate pieces of paper. Again, distribute and students have to move around the room to pair the halves. This can also be done statically, with students reading out their half and people putting their hands up if they think that they have the matching answer.

2. Sequencing – write a paragraph intended to stimulate discussion on to a sheet of paper. Cut it up and distribute to students. They have to work together to reconstruct the paragraph on the board.

Aim to make reading an interactive task so that students can explore the meanings and tasks as a team.

Engaging the students with the starting activity

There are some effective lesson starters that directly challenge your students to focus on the topic to be covered:

- Ask students for key ideas from last lesson (with their books closed) and collate as a collective mind map on the board

- Ask students what they already know about the lesson content. Put this on to a mind map on the board

- List student predictions about the content of the lesson, given the topic

These approaches boost student self-esteem as you are giving status to their ideas and prior knowledge.

Creative ways to use a lesson title

To encourage students to think about a topic, it is sometimes useful to ask them to reflect on the lesson title.

- Put the lesson title on the board as a cryptic question. Invite students to guess the topic of the lesson
- Start with a game of hangman, the phrase being filled in becoming the lesson focus and title
- Add further depth by linking the lesson focus/content to a key skill, eg using bullet points. On the board put the focus and, in a thought bubble, put the skill they will be using. So, if a lesson is based on making something in DT, then part of the student responses should be written as bullet points. You could encourage colleagues to choose the same key skill for their lessons at some point in the week, to reinforce the key skill across subjects

These approaches will give variety to mundane everyday tasks that children face lesson to lesson. They will help make your lesson interestingly different from others.

Using homework as an active starter

A good starter can be set up in a previous homework. This will help link a run of lessons and create a sense of narrative or progression in your students' minds.

- Pair and share – split the class in two and give them a different homework task each. Start the next lesson by pairing up the students to share each other's findings

- A simple approach is to ask for pictures linked to the next lesson. Make sure that you have glue and a couple of sheets of sugar paper. Put the blank paper on the wall. When students arrive get them to glue their picture on to the sheets

- Use 'show and tell', where students bring in things to show and discuss with the rest of the class

Using homework to build a lesson

It is important to give homework status so that students will engage with it purposefully. The following starter is ideal for this:

- On the board, outline the key points of the last lesson
- Ask the students to add on new information found out for homework
- Then get students to select the most important new piece of information
- Usually two or three points will be identified. Draw this up in a table as a discussion point/memory and revision aid

This starter can then be developed in several ways, incorporating homework into the main part of the lesson.

Challenge Your Comfort Zones

 Starting Out

 Asking the Right Questions ◀

 Active Learning

 Making Technology Work for You

 Creative Lesson Ideas

Revision Aids

Building a Sense of Teamwork

Asking the Right Questions

Get your students to Bloom

As a classroom teacher a lot of your time is spent asking students to respond to questions. The theoretical base to good questioning technique lies somewhere between Regan (of *The Sweeney*) or perhaps Phil Mitchell, and the work of Benjamin Bloom in the 1950s.

Bloom identified different orders of questions that led to different levels of response, from simple recall of knowledge to more complicated synthesis and evaluation. He found that over 80% of teacher questions required students to respond only at the simplest 'recall of knowledge' level.

So, by skilful variation of question type you, as a teacher, have a powerful tool for moving students to more sophisticated ways of interacting with knowledge. You should be able to use this chapter to creatively incorporate the ideas of Bloom – with maybe a touch of Regan/Mitchell – into your classroom activities.

Using Bloom's taxonomy to develop work

You can use Bloom's creative **question cues** to develop students' engagement with, and development of, learning opportunities, eg by planning a lesson or run of lessons building on increasingly higher order questioning/enquiry.

SKILL	QUESTION CUES
KNOWLEDGE	**define, describe, list**
COMPREHENSION	**compare, contrast, explain**
APPLICATION	**select, use, experiment**
ANALYSIS	**examine, investigate, rank**
SYNTHESIS	**develop, rearrange, reorganise, predict**
EVALUATION	**judge, assess, appraise**

A stepped approach could be *'describe'* followed by *'explain'* and *'compare'* followed by *'predict/develop.'* So:
Describe the food, **explain** how it was made, **compare** it with other food, and then **develop** ways to improve the food.
Describe the experiment, **explain** the process, **compare** with another experiment, **predict** what might happen if variables are changed.

Using Bloom to create ladders for learning $\boxed{?}$

Aim to move students towards more complicated work by using carefully selected question cues.

- Use *'Who?'* *'What?'* *'Where?'* and simple *'Which one?'* questions as a starting point. You can then record the student responses on the board as a learning anchor

- Develop these into explanation style questions such as, *'What does this mean?'* and *'What might be happening?'*

- End with evaluative questions such as, *'Which is the best?'*, *'What is most likely?'*, or predictive questions such as, *'How might this…?'* and *'What would test this…?'*

Use this kind of questioning to build ladders for learning. It can really help if you keep the same rhythm in your questions so that your students get used to moving from simple statements to more complicated responses. Explain to the students what you are doing, and work with them so that they can build their own question ladders.

Using activities linked to Bloom

Instead of questions, you can use *tasks* to lead students to higher outcomes, building from simple activities to more complicated tasks.

- Start with simple conversion of content into posters, newspaper articles or cartoons
- Move to more difficult tasks such as speeches, games, video presentations and songs
- Finish, for example, with debates, written evaluation of materials, rewriting of content for a different audience, and alternative uses of knowledge gained

This will allow genuine group work, as students are able to contribute at their level and also develop as the tasks move on. Your students will begin to learn from each other and you will be fostering a sense of teamwork within the learning experience.

Avoiding pitfalls

When you invite student verbal responses there are two types of questions to avoid:

- The one that kills further development by needing a yes/no or correct/incorrect answer. *Unless it is intended*
- The question the student can't engage with, and which results in them sitting in embarrassed silence

You need to make students feel that they can all contribute to a discussion, but it's not always easy to avoid developing a 'discussion clique' where a handful of students dominate. Using groups to come up with answers is a good way to involve the quieter students, especially if you have a 'rotating chair' approach when the time comes to contribute, ie each student gets to feed back points.

Even so, some students simply are too shy to speak in front of the whole class – make sure you go to these students during the lesson so that they can talk to you personally. You can then build their confidence by introducing points they have made along the lines of, *'Sophie made a good point to me earlier…'* and you tell the class.

Powerful words

Your most powerful words as a teacher when interacting with students are:

Student skills development

By asking the right questions you should lead students to activities that allow them to develop creatively as learners.

In a run of lessons have you allowed the students to:

Reproduce ideas/information in their own style?	❏
Compare and contrast ideas and information?	❏
Develop problem solving skills by applying new information?	❏
Analyse and break down ideas and information?	❏
Use new ideas to draw conclusions or offer extensions?	❏
Assess, rank and evaluate new knowledge?	❏

Sometimes **looking at the skills** will allow you to **plan** your lesson to **focus on the right questions and activities**.

Challenge Your
Comfort Zones

 Starting
Out

 Asking the
Right Questions

 Active
Learning

 Making
Technology
Work for You

 Creative
Lesson Ideas

Revision
Aids

 Building a
Sense of
Teamwork

Active Learning

Creating an Active Learning Environment

Basic principles

Active learning can energise your classroom and bring the fun element into teaching. It gives students a sense of responsibility for what goes on and makes their ideas and actions central to the learning experience. As the teacher, you can also be active in how you present otherwise routine classroom tasks. To build creative lessons that support active learning, consider the following in your planning:

1. How to **activate previous learning**. For example, using mind maps at the start of a lesson to summarise earlier work will help students link their learning.

2. Ensuring that the work you set is challenging and that you allow students to **work in groups** to complete tasks. Sharing knowledge and ideas is a good way to learn creatively. One effective technique is to use sorting exercises – using pictures, phrases or tasks – where a group of students have to select a few from a number of options linked to a line of enquiry or topic. The process of selecting and eliminating through arguing a case and then explaining the choices encourages active learning.

Creating an Active Learning Environment

Basic principles

3. How to **encourage metacognition** (ie thinking about learning). One powerful way is to ask students how they will tackle a task/solve a problem. Similarly, ask them to review how they undertook a task and how they could improve their approach next time they are set a similar problem.

4. Asking students to **convert information from one type to another**. Changing text into pictures, visual images into discussion, paragraphs into bullet points, sound into pictures and so on are all excellent ways of fostering active learning and creativity. The challenge of looking at information and presenting it in a new way is demanding and engaging.

5. **Providing scaffolding/ladders for learning**. If you break a task into chunks so that students can move from one step to another, from simple to complex/easy to difficult, your students will over time be able to climb the ladder independently. Using questions/tasks based on Bloom's Taxonomy will help. (See pages 35-36)

When and why

If you set up active learning activities in your lessons, you and your class can work as a team. Students will more readily engage with their learning if they can participate in the delivery of their lesson. Encourage this by giving them specific parts of the lesson to deliver. Keep the timing and focus very tight to ensure pace and purpose for the activity. Lesson starters and closers are ideal to give over to students, as they encourage the skills of summary and synthesis.

5 Key Points

* _____
* _____
* _____
* _____
* _____

Using TV as a model

Television soap operas are a good planning guide. *Students remember reasonably complicated and multiple plot lines* due to the way these programmes use **reinforcement, recap, and cliffhangers**. Model your lessons along these lines. Reinforcement and recap become 'starters' and cliffhangers are useful 'plenaries' which then work as starters next time.

This approach also allows a sense of drama to be given to more abstract content such as mathematical and scientific equations, ending lessons with unsolved puzzles and formulae that will be resolved the next lesson. Science practicals are particularly good for engendering this approach, the experiments being the reinforcement, and the outcomes the cliffhangers. What is important is how you, as a teacher, set up the delivery – a larger than life, slightly 'hammy' approach rarely fails.

Using script writing and role-play

Make students' leisure interests work for you as a teacher.

- Use film techniques to help you – get students to storyboard the important aspects of the lesson. Reduce key facts to single statements with accompanying pictures. In time ask students to identify key facts and storyboard them

- Ask students to write lesson content up as if pitching for a TV advert. If you teach a practical subject, you can get the students to put together adverts for the equipment they are using, based on their own use of them

- Ask the class how various soap characters would view the work being done. Pick a range of characters to use, but include a couple of very dim ones. This will allow students to hang their own difficulties on the dim soap character, and allow you to help by asking the students how they would make the character understand

Find inspiration in quiz shows

You can use TV quiz shows as lesson templates. Using modern shows will create a sense of familiarity in the students' minds and help the learning, but older programmes can be useful too. You probably have favourite quiz shows of your own – see how you can adapt them for use in the class.
Here are a few ideas:

"Specialist subject: simultaneous equations at GCSE"

- The old show *'Runaround'* can be adapted to get students to respond to questions – post different answers in different parts of the room and students choose which one to stand by

- *'The Weakest Link'* – focusing questions on your subject area is an ideal way to motivate smaller or less able classes

- Hot-seating as in *'Mastermind'* is also productive

Encourage the students to invent their own television game show based on your lesson content. The students can then develop this as a quiz game that you can use each year.

Working with character cards

Some students find it difficult when asked to respond to questions as themselves. You can set up character cards to help them engage with this kind of task in role.

- Make the character cards simple for ease of use – they could be emotional character prompts – for example, how would an impatient or angry person react to the lesson content?
- Set up prompt cards to allow students to explore different viewpoints. For example, how would a deaf/blind/different language speaking student be best taught the content of the lesson?

These approaches will also help students develop an understanding of other people's viewpoints.

Angry hats and empathy glasses

Using simple props can encourage students to see ideas from various perspectives. They can also introduce a sense of fun into the learning processes – always a positive thing.

Angry hats. Buy two or three hats from a charity shop. Label them with contrasting emotions or personality types. The simplest are an angry hat and a happy hat. The student wearing the hat has to respond in the manner of the label on the hat.

Empathy glasses. Make a big prop of a pair of glasses. They empower the wearer to see things or examine ideas from another person's point of view.

Whose round is it?

You can encourage students to interact with a range of materials by making the lesson competitive, with some rewards for the winning teams.

- As a one-off, set up a lesson like a pub quiz with the class divided into teams participating in different rounds to get a final score
- Give the students round headings suggesting an activity or approach, (eg one round could be called *'Fill in the Blanks'* another *'Odd One Out'*) and run the rounds once a fortnight or so to set up the league approach

If the teams are kept the same, a league system can be set up for the year. You can display the quiz league in your classroom to provide a competitive focus and an interactive display. You could also allocate roles within the teams, eg score recorder or team captain to increase a sense of responsibility within the class.

These approaches will help your students to build a sense of teamwork, as well as sharpening their research and synthesis skills.

Convert the work

You have almost certainly, at some point in your teaching life, used the approach which converts lesson content to newspaper pages. Here are some variations on the theme that you could try out with your students.

- Create cartoons – both strip and single frames of key learning points

- Get students to concentrate knowledge into newsflashes/headlines

Convert the work

- Covert information to text messages, eg: **H8 grt kng 6wvs**

- Write a soap opera script, making key lesson information into characters who interact, eg: ***Imagine the sodium family at home avoiding dangers, then the water salesman calls.***

If you do use the newspaper approach, try setting up 'newsdesks': give students the information in small chunks in real time, so that they have to amend their report/front page as more information comes in. This works well if you use A3 paper as the page, with strips/columns of blank paper that students can write on to stick over information that has been superseded by more up-to-date details. Increase the pressure with a time deadline for final copy.

"News just coming through..."

**Challenge Your
Comfort Zones**

**Starting
Out**

**Asking the
Right Questions**

**Active
Learning**

 **Making
Technology
Work for You**

 **Creative
Lesson Ideas**

 **Revision
Aids**

 **Building a
Sense of
Teamwork**

Making
Technology Work
for You

From chalkboard to interactive whiteboard

As a teacher you are often pressurised to use the latest ICT whizbang gadget in your teaching. ICT as a tool for learning works best if the students are put at the centre of the technology, and when the ICT doesn't slow down or get in the way of lesson content delivery.

If you have an interactive whiteboard it is good if the students can use it more than you. But the same goes for the good old-fashioned chalkboard – students can come up and write/draw on it as easily as they can access the interactive whiteboard. It is also important not to lose sight of what good memory prompts all boards are – it is all very well losing yourself in virtual flipcharts and animated sequences, but don't forget most students really appreciate the board to show lesson title, instructions, and key word definitions.

ICT works best if you see it as a support for your teaching, rather than as a vehicle for your teaching. Sometimes it will be a useful creative tool, at other times pen and paper will do just as well.

Engaging students with videos/DVDs

To maximise the effect of video/DVD use in the classroom you need to give careful thought to the structure of the delivery. Also be sensitive to the attention span of students, and work with them to interact with the material, rather than simply observe it.

- Use targeted viewing – give students things to look out for. For example, have students looking out for particular individuals, interactions, scenes, phrases or camera angles

Engaging students with videos/DVDs

- Press pause and get students to predict what will happen. This can be grounded in factual videos, for example ones showing science experiments or sports activities, as well as fictional videos for subjects such as English

- Give groups of students specific parts of the video to follow – they then write up as rest of class watch their bit. All groups then report back at the end. Alternatively, all students watch but are given 10 minute slots to report back on to really focus their attention

This approach will help you to focus students directly on a specific watching task. It will also help them discuss the material at the end of the showing, thereby helping reinforce content.

Student interaction with a video/DVD

You can embed video material firmly into a lesson if it is broken into viewing sections and interactive activities.

- If question sheets are to be used, set them up to follow about 10 minute viewing chunks, ie watch for ten minutes, stop, deploy question sheet. Or let students read them prior to video showing

- Stop the film so that students can discuss a practical application of what they have just seen

- Students pick up from where the video/DVD has stopped by role-playing what they have seen

- Students critically evaluate each section for ease of learning, and offer alternative scenes

- Turn off the sound and get students to write a script. If you are brave, detune the picture but keep the sound and get students to imagine what the visuals could be

The key is to watch in segments of no longer than ten minutes, and then for you to tightly focus the follow-up activity.

Filming and role-play

Role-play can be a fun way of engaging students in a learning activity. It also allows abstract ideas to be explored in an active way. If the role-play is to be filmed, there are simple ways that you can enhance the learning experience.

- Don't just film the drama, encourage a question and answer session of the performers at the end and film that too
- If key phrases arise in the course of the role-play, put them on the board. Take a still shot of the list at the end, keeping a permanent discussion point
- Watch the recording with the class, asking them to look for key points in the drama, pressing pause to explore the issues raised

You will learn a lot more from role-play if you break it down as outlined above, but don't forget the value of role-play as fun just to give yourself and the students a chance to relax and blow off steam!

Using computers

There are some very effective ways of encouraging students to use ICT, but as a teacher you need to ask yourself key questions:

- How will using computers enhance this task?
- Am I running this task to add value to my subject, or simply to allow students to use the computer room?
- Is this task time-efficient if done on computers?

It is easy to use computers simply as word processors – and certainly for drafting and redrafting they are an invaluable tool. But where the aim is to encourage skills of research, synthesis, and independent study careful planning and preparation are necessary for successful results.

Using computers

A simple creative approach

There are many useful subject-specific applications available to schools which go beyond the scope of this book, but here is a simple idea to enable your students to use computers independently to research, select, synthesise, and present.

The A4 Fact sheet
- Give students focus/line of enquiry
- Students set up page in Word or similar with focus heading
- Select relevant picture from web search/clip art/ CDROM to match focus
- Cut and stick into Word page
- Students then write under the picture five bullet points of information relevant to the fact sheet. If information is cut and pasted from the Internet, it must be reworded by the students
- Print out sheet

This will allow the students to work creatively with the volume of information available through the Internet, while keeping work focused on your subject. You can then put fact sheets together and photocopy them as resources for the class, and next year's students.

Using overhead projectors

Overhead projectors are a good stimulus if you let students add information to them. You can set up a short piece of text, picture, formula or cloze exercise on the transparency and students can come up and write around the focus and see their work instantly displayed on the screen. Another approach is to give out blank transparencies and ask students to create their own linked to the lesson task/content.

OHPs also work extremely well as spotlights for hot-seating activities!

Digital cameras

A quick and easy way to add status to a lesson is to take digital pictures of the class as they work and then e-mail the pictures to the students own in-school addresses, or print them off for students to stick in their books next to their work. This will help them remember the lesson and its content.

A more complicated way is to group students in your lessons as media teams, with each team responsible for taking pictures of, and reporting on, one lesson a half term. For that lesson, the three or four in the media team whose turn it is, interact with the other students as they work, rather than doing the tasks themselves.

Making 'new' technology work for you

In recent years the technology available to support creative teaching has developed almost beyond recognition. Interactive whiteboards have changed how lessons can be delivered, and a range of new technologies such as internet-ready mobile phones and mp3/4 players have changed how students can interact in lessons and undertake their learning.

The following pages provide ideas for using these new technologies creatively both in the classroom and beyond.

Virtual Learning Environments

The Government target for all schools to have a Virtual Learning Environment (VLE) in place by 2010 hastened the growth of VLEs and MLEs (Managed Learning Environments) in schools.

Both VLEs and MLEs are developments of the old intranets that many schools had in place at the start of the 21st century. A VLE is a 'stand alone' environment not linked to any other school systems (such as the schools information management system, SIMS); the MLE is a more all-encompassing environment in which all school systems are 'under one roof'. In effect, an MLE is a virtual school. It contains all kinds of information ranging from student data to virtual classrooms. These virtual classrooms, with their facility for interactivity, offer a range of creative teaching opportunities. They also offer opportunities for teachers to work smarter and save time.

Virtual classrooms

You can set up your own virtual classroom for each group you teach. Students can then log on and visit the room. What you put in it is largely up to you. For example, you can:

- Create discussion forums where students can post their ideas/generate debate
- Use information containers to inform students about, say, examination dates and papers, with hyperlinks to exam board web pages
- Post your lesson plans and resources so that students can access and develop work at home/outside of the lesson
- Construct polls for students to register their views. One department uses a poll to ask students whether they definitely want to take the subject at GCSE, are thinking about taking it, or are definitely not taking it. This helps department planning long before GCSE options are actually taken.
- Set up ideas forums. I have used these successfully by asking students to post ideas for lesson activities to feed into my planning
- Post your entire interactive whiteboard lesson as a pdf for students to view at home

Virtual classrooms

In both VLEs and MLEs you can set and receive student work. There are also virtual mark books you can use. The ability to contact students via their virtual mail address means you can chase up and monitor tasks set via the Learning Environment. You can also feed back marks and comments in the same way. Homework can now be sent electronically to the VLE/MLE to be marked and students can access their grades and feedback from home

Projects can be set, eg you can set tasks and upload pictures for students to view as stimuli and insert hyperlinks to guide students to good websites. This is particularly useful for younger students who are just learning to engage with websites.

Once the virtual classrooms have been set up, the time-saving benefit to the teacher is clear. All you need to do in following years is tweak what is already there. With lesson materials and other resources in place, planning time is reduced to adapting what you have for different students rather than the time-consuming starting from scratch.

Yacapaca and Googledocs

The free sites Yacapaca and Googledocs offer creative opportunities for setting tasks and saving time.

At **Yacapaca.com** teachers across the country post tasks for students to access from home. You can assign any of these to your students and can also set up your own activities for other teachers to use. The site generates a mark book and the vast majority of material is marked automatically.

It is useful for setting multiple choice quizzes to support learning or exam revision. Students might be required, for instance, to identify key words, definitions and phrases. Automatic marking aids the students and saves you having to laboriously mark a pile of revision tests.

Googledocs

Googledocs.com is useful for setting up student reviews. You can create a questionnaire online comprising a range of types of question, eg:

- A 'tick box' style question asking which areas students are happiest with
- A rating question with a scale of 1-10 about enjoyment of the course
- A free text box where students can evaluate which parts of the course they would like more support with

You then link the questionnaire to your VLE/MLE for students to complete. When you open the document in your area, student responses are collated on a spreadsheet. The process is straightforward and efficient. It saves you having to juggle multiple sheets of paper and it gives a quick, easily-read overview of how things are going.

Mobile Phones

A number of schools are now taking the more creative step of allowing students to have their mobile phones as a learning aid rather than banning them from the classroom altogether. It is a thorny issue, but phones can be used to support creative lesson activities, from simple picture-taking to accessing the internet.
Here are some examples:

- In one lesson students were encouraged to use their phones as part of a homework to research 'Civil Rights' in America. In the following lesson they downloaded video footage and music from their phones to the school computer system to put together presentations

- In an Art lesson students were encouraged to use their phones to photograph different textured materials as part of a project. Once again, images were then downloaded and used as supporting resources for the subsequent work

- Students were tasked to find music to accompany poetry they had discussed in an English lesson. The music was downloaded to phones and shared in class

YouTube

YouTube, with its video clips on just about any topic you can name, is a godsend for teachers. It opens up a world of opportunities beyond the old style 'show a video' approach, eg: a suffragette lesson incorporating YouTube footage of a newsreel of Emily Davison's death; a citizenship lesson using footage from party political broadcasts; a PE lesson using clips from the Olympic Games; and music lessons using clips of musicians playing different types of piano music to demonstrate the instrument's range.

In one school:

- A YouTube clip was used in a history lesson to teach students how to Charleston!
- In an English lesson students were given the key word 'satire' and had to find clips to amplify the concept
- Food Technology students found clips of cookery programmes from 1950 – 2000. They were asked to explain how the style and techniques had changed, and then to choose one style for their own presentation to the class

Interactive whiteboards/data projectors

Most schools now have interactive whiteboards. The creative opportunities are endless. A typical whiteboard lesson could include:

- A short video clip from YouTube to introduce the topic
- A hyperlink to a web page with further information and images
- A page of tasks decorated with relevant images cut and pasted from the internet
- A click and drag task where students come to the board and move information around
- A blank mind map as a plenary. Students come up and write onto it key points learnt during the lesson

As a teacher, an interactive whiteboard allows you to create a lesson, store it, and then amend it for future use. You can easily access and display the previous lesson on the board for reconsideration or reinforcement next time you see a class.

Podcasts

The portable technology that comes as mp3/4 players has many creative applications both inside and outside the classroom. Students can download podcasts to their players, eg for revision purposes, or they can make their own in lesson time:

- One colleague used her laptop to record a round table discussion among her 'A' level students who then downloaded the recording as a podcast on to their mp3 players to listen to as part of their further study
- One GCSE teacher made his own revision podcasts summarising key points. He then allowed students to download them for individual use
- Several students made their own podcasts of key revision topics for GCSE and downloaded them to play as they travelled to school on the bus
- A number of sites offer pre-recorded podcasts for students. Check out www.bbc.co.uk/schools/gcsebitesize and www.amazinggrades.com

It's easy to feel overwhelmed by constant advances in technology, especially if you were around before the electronic/digital revolution, but if you view podcasts as the latest version of 'taping stuff', then all kinds of creative options present themselves.

Afterword

New technologies can easily outpace teacher confidence and comfort.
Arguably, the best way to combat this is to take off your teaching hat in the classroom and ask your pupils to suggest how *they* might use the technology. (I have found that students make a good deal more sense when explaining how to use 'new' technology than a two hour after school INSET session!)

As a 'forty-something' teacher, my most creative use of technology in lessons has come after talking things through with my students. The positive effect on the classroom dynamic when students see that you value their ideas and knowledge as a key part of creative teaching is an added advantage.

Creative Lesson Ideas

Creative kernels

The following pages are intended to support you in the delivery of creative lessons. As such they are snapshots of different lesson ideas that can be adapted freely for your own use:

Oh I say!

One minute tasks to introduce/close topics are actually quite stretching for students. You can build up to them by first getting each student to say one thing that highlights key learning points. Then get groups of students to quickly plan a verbal summary of part of the lesson and deliver it.

This will get your students into the habit of analysing and identifying important learning points, as well as 'chunking' work for revision. You can develop what students say by rooting summaries as mind maps or bullet points for students to have as revision points or memory aids.

The deliberately obscure game

Students have to make five statements about a topic. The statements must be true, but obscure or cryptic. After each statement other students write down their guesses. With each statement students can amend their guesses, but points decline as more clues are given.

Guess after first statement =10 marks, then 7, 5, 3, and finally 1 mark for guess after the fifth statement.

The two winners at the lesson-end are the questioner who has the fewest points scored against them, and the student with the most points from their guesses of other people's topics. You should take part in the guesses, but be prepared to take a bit of stick if the students outwit you!

This is a very effective tool to stimulate thinking around a subject.

The lite lesson approach!

One challenging idea is to get your students to reduce lesson content right down to the bare bones.

- Reduce a page of text to two key points
- Summarise a long practical experiment into three bullet points
- Sum up what has been learned in no more than 30 words
- Demonstrate a key learning point as a mime
- Turn an equation into a statement
- Turn a statement into a flowchart or equation

This will encourage the students to creatively break down their work for easy recollection.

Big it up

You can use the mirror image of the preceding tasks: give the students a brief stimulus and ask them to expand it.

- A couple of brief statements have to be developed into a paragraph of text
- Abstract ideas have to be enlarged into a role-play
- Bullet points have to be combined with student-selected visual materials to produce a mock text book page

This will challenge your students to explore and enlarge basic key facts. You can use these tasks to help students with their extended writing and support whole school literacy.

Quizzicals

Get your students to write quizzes for the year below them. These can later be deployed as starters or closers of lessons, or at ends of terms. One simple method is to distribute textbooks and students have to come up with 20 questions and answers. This actively encourages research skills by stealth!

For all subjects the quiz can be more creatively structured by giving out answers. Students then work out as many ways of getting to the answer as possible, eg:

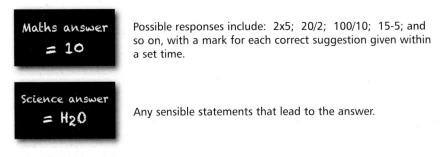

Maths answer = 10

Possible responses include: 2x5; 20/2; 100/10; 15-5; and so on, with a mark for each correct suggestion given within a set time.

Science answer = H_2O

Any sensible statements that lead to the answer.

Board games, not bored students!

You can help your students understand difficult content by encouraging the conversion of information into board games. If you use simple right or wrong options for some questions on the boards, students will soon learn the right answer. All you need is A3 paper, coloured A4, scissors, glue, and dice.

Don't be afraid to have a lesson where the students simply play their games.

- You can get your students to play each other's games and evaluate their degree of difficulty/usefulness for revision

- If you store the games, other classes can use them as revision tools

This works extremely well as a GCSE revision technique, and engages younger classes well too.

Let's Predict

Predictive exercises are very good for creatively engaging students in lesson tasks.

Guess the fact envelope

In an envelope enclose a piece of paper on which you have written the main fact from the lesson. Show students the envelope. They have to write down one guess at what the piece of paper says. Those who match yours are rewarded. This can be extended to asking students to justify their choices before you finally reveal yours.

'Spot the error' game

Tell students that something you will tell them in the next five minutes will contain an error. The students then have to listen/make notes for the next five minutes before teaming up with textbooks to see if they can find your mistake. This works just as well on worksheets.

Examine it

You can support your students in their examination preparations by encouraging them to engage directly with the activities that will help them maximise their success.

- Turn classes into exam boards – students use materials to make their own exam paper, with questions and a mark scheme. This will put your students at the heart of the examination process and allow them to look at their work in a new light

- Cut paper to sizes that fit the general length of answers that you want. This is very effective at GCSE to stop students overwriting small mark answers, and underwriting longer ones. It also helps the students with timing in exams

- Use chess clocks or egg timers to help students write to a time deadline

These ideas will help your students deal with the **purpose** and **pressure** of the exams.

That gets my vote

You can encourage student interaction in discussion by giving them props and cues that allow them to access the arguments more freely than just by 'hands up'.

- Use rolled-up 'voting rods' for students to vote on topics or show understanding. Red for 'against/disagree', green for 'yes/agree'. These can be used individually, or given to a group which then has to discuss its response to a question

If you put the student responses on to the board in the same colour as the voting rod – for example all 'against' arguments in red – it will help students to remember the points made.

Yes, no, don't know

If students have a fixed view about something, use the following approach to challenge ideas. It's a quick way to start a discussion.

- Have 'for', 'against' and 'undecided' tables in a lesson when you have a discussion. Sit the students at the desks and make sure they adopt the attitude of the table, not their own view. This will stretch the more able and support the less confident

Root good ideas and points raised on to the board for writing down at the end of the discussion so that the learning is fixed for revision and future development. This tactic can also allow you to give students a 'time out': if arguments become a bit heated, ask them to write down the points you have put on the board. The process allows your students an opportunity for reflection, and lets them then move the discussion on.

Working groups

Sometimes breaking classes into groups causes arguments and problems that ruin the atmosphere for the task that follows. There are times when you will need to engineer groupings, but when you don't, try these ideas to set up groups:

- Just number the tables 1-5 and count the students in 1-5, telling them to sit at the table with their number. Preparing numbered cards for your students and tables makes this method even more effective

- Try the fruit bowl approach. Give each student the name of one of five or six fruits. They form their groups by linking up with one of each of the other different fruits

"Hee Hee, Sir's gone bananas!"

- Draw lots linked to table location

Creative Brainstorming

To encourage pupils to work together and think around a subject, try the ideas on this page. Students who find whole-class brainstorming daunting are more able to share their ideas in the smaller groups used for these two activities.

Double mind maps
Ask students, in pairs or small groups, to create two mind maps for two related subjects and then look at where the two overlap. This helps them to see and understand similarities and differences, eg between two animals or plants in Science, in how two characters react within a story for English or Drama, or in two different events in History.

Table tennis trios
Organise students into threes and give them a topic. One student writes the mind map as the other two take quick-fire turns to say something linked to the subject. Then swap two of the roles so a different person takes over the mapping and the scribe can join in with ideas. This is a quick and interactive way to brainstorm information.

Brainstraining

These three ideas are aimed at stretching students during group work. The aim is to challenge them to use their memory and to stimulate discussion and research.

1. **Test the collective memory**. Organise pupils into groups and show them a picture/diagram/section of text, giving them about 30 seconds to study it. Send each group away with a sheet of paper, asking them to write down (or draw or sketch if it's a picture or map) what they have just seen. After a few minutes, give them the source material to check how good their collective memory was. A useful extension is to ask pupils to explain the various recall tricks they used.

2. **The runaway train**. In groups pupils write down a piece of information linked to the topic they are studying. They then add two more pieces of information, then a further four, then eight, doubling up all the time. When their memory fails or knowledge is exhausted, allow them to switch to further research using books and the internet.

3. **Leave it out**. Give students 30 seconds to look at a selection of information, eg a group of statements; a series of equations; a collection of objects or images. Remove one item. Pupils look again for 15 seconds and work out what's missing.

Plenaries

A good lesson conclusion will sum up the learning achieved, highlight significant parts of the lesson, and set up what is to come next time. This can be entirely teacher-led, but there are other creative approaches to closing down a lesson.

Mirror the starter

Say the lesson started with a mind map outlining what the students already knew about the content, conclude with a mind map summing up what new information has been added.

Plenaries

A creative plenary will also provide the students you teach with a simple revision point. For the less able the summary task will highlight the key learning points, and allow access to them quickly and easily.

Fascinating fact box

At the close of the lesson get students to write down the most interesting/strange fact from the lesson. Start the next lesson by collating some on to a mind map.

Gimme five

At the end of a lesson students have to list five key things learned. Make them into a display, perhaps to be discussed as a starter next time around.

These approaches will also provide students with revision points in their books.

Plenaries

Accustom students to synthesising lesson content by writing short lists of the main ideas covered in a lesson. Three points are plenty to encourage students to overview the lesson. Some variations on the theme:

We the jury

Students identify their number one choices and then take part in a class vote to see what the class thinks is the most important thing learned in the lesson.

Crystal gazing

Write down on a piece of paper the main points of the lesson and invite students to guess what you have written down, and why. This can be adapted in several ways – one that works well is to draw a crystal ball on the board and invite students up to write their guesses around it.

This will let you either develop the closing activity by asking the class to contribute in a discussion of the key facts covered, or provide you with a neat starter activity for the next lesson.

Plenaries

It is a good idea for you to have an active closing activity 'up your sleeve'. This can be made more versatile if you can think of a similar but quiet version, eg:

Active conclusion – pair the students up to do a quick 'newsflash' feedback to the class. The students have to verbally report back on the lesson, but only have 30 seconds in which to speak.

Quieter variation – students write an encyclopaedia entry, based on the lesson's main facts, but they can only use 30 words.

This pairing of opposites gives you more tools in your teaching toolkit and allows you to respond to circumstances.

Plenaries to help literacy

You can aim some plenaries at supporting whole-school policies such as literacy, while also generating useful teaching aids for your classroom.

Give it a gloss

Encourage students to select five words from the lesson and construct a glossary at the back of their books. These can be used as a spelling test lesson starter next time. This activity can also be used if one student spells and then another gives a definition or context for the word.

Plenaries to help literacy

Word wall

Set up an active 'word wall' – an area of the room where new words are posted by students at the end of a lesson.

These approaches allow you to introduce new vocabulary into the lesson and to highlight key subject-specific words and phrases.

Hyperbole

Paradox

Bathos

Oxymoron

Juxtaposition

Metaphor

Connecting with the next lesson

To **reinforce the sense of narrative** needed for students to **connect** their learning, use a plenary to look ahead to future work. This can be a simple teacher-led outline of what will be done next time or more involved student prediction based on what has just been studied. Predictive exercises like this reinforce learning and stretch the students to think beyond the limits of the current lesson.

Another simple connecting activity is for your students to write the next lesson's title into their book. This helps link lessons and provides you with a ready-made starting point next time around.

This approach allows interested students to read around the subject independently or to voluntarily bring relevant materials to the next lesson to show you.

Connecting with the next lesson

You can extend the range of your lesson-linking by looking for active and peaceful versions of activities as described on page 92. The following ideas can be used to link one lesson to another – but one version is far more hectic than the other!

Active link – students write questions they want addressed on paper and then turn them into aeroplanes that they launch around the room. You can collect them and use a few as a lesson starter next time.

Peaceful link – you have a post box on your desk. Students write their queries and post them for your consideration between lessons.

 Challenge Your
Comfort Zones

Starting
Out

 Asking the
Right Questions

Active
Learning

 Making
Technology Work
for You

Creative
Lesson Ideas

 Revision
Aids

 Building a
Sense of
Teamwork

Revision Aids

Effective revision modelling

There is no point teaching engaging and creative lessons if students aren't shown how to retain information from them!

Revision needs to be taught to your classes. To encourage students to use a range of techniques, eg mind maps; posters; audio tapes; podcasts; 'new' technologies such as mobile phones; mind pegs, you need to incorporate these approaches into your everyday teaching.

Mind pegs

A mind peg is information that the students already know, on to which they can connect new knowledge. You can set up various ways for students to hang the new knowledge on to the existing mind peg. Typical mind pegs can be a variety of stimuli including:

- Family members
- Songs
- Route to school
- Layout of student's house
- Musicians in a group

Mind pegs in action

- Get students to write lyrics/raps based on lesson content to songs/music they already know

- To root more abstract ideas, try linking existing memory of friends or family with the target knowledge. Get students to imagine their friend wearing a t-shirt with the key information on, or break up the information and imagine a family member carrying each piece

- Key information can be linked to key points on the route to school or family home. Students visualise the ideas as they pass each location

The possibilities for mind pegs are endless; familiarise your classes with the technique then encourage students to find their own pegs and practise using them.

Mind pegs and numbers

Mathematical formulae and scientific equations can be effectively remembered by the use of mnemonics as mind pegs, eg:

- **N**aughty **C**hildren **l**ick salt
- **H**arry **2** **O**verweight for water

It is possible to build up quite complicated formulae using this idea, but always look for some kind of memorable narrative.

Mind pegs and dates

Encourage students to convert numbers to visual images to help them grasp information. For some students, this is a good way to remember dates. The first example uses number of letters per word to encode the date and the second uses the shapes of the images:

- A motorbike goes fast (imagine Hitler riding it back to Germany)= 1944
  A=1 motorbike=9 goes=4 fast=4

- A swan gave two rings to a flag (on the twin towers)= 2001
  2=swan 0 0= two rings 1=flag

The more surreal the image, the easier it is to remember.

Ideas to help visual learners

Visual learners tend to favour activities that are linked to images. Encourage visual learners to:

- Make flashcards of key revision points, with a picture on one side and brief text underneath
- Design posters of the main ideas/facts
- Create coloured mind maps
- As a teacher you can help the visual learner by linking colour and shapes to key information points and by deliberately using phrases that stimulate 'the mind's eye', eg *'When did we last see this?'*; *'How would this appear to you?'*; *'Let's build on what we saw last lesson'*

Ideas to help auditory learners

You can support effective revision for auditory learners by a range of techniques linked to hearing. Encourage auditory learners to:

- Make audio tapes or podcasts to play back on Walkmans and iPods
- Explain ideas verbally to a partner
- Take part in discussions aimed at ordering their thoughts
- Summarise information in their own words

Ideas to help kinaesthetic learners

More active revision can suit kinaesthetic learners, but there is also a need to address the written elements of examinations in all that they do. Encourage these kinds of learner to:

- Sort revision cards into order
- Ground work into mind maps
- Make revision posters and keep changing their display location
- Move around to revise in different rooms during a revision session

You need to give kinaesthetic learners opportunities to acclimatise to sitting still in an examination context, so practise short bursts of inaction throughout the run of lessons.

Colour coding

Linking abstract ideas or arguments to colour helps to anchor information. Students associate the colour with the information. One simple approach is traffic light coding:

- RED – link to 'stop/hinder' or 'negative' or 'dangerous' or 'against' or 'hot'
- AMBER – link to 'join' or 'balanced/neutral' or 'changing' or 'unsure'
- GREEN – link to 'go/progress' or 'positive' or 'safe' or 'certain/for' or 'cold'

Use colour as background on to which related information is recorded, or write parts of the information in the appropriate colour.

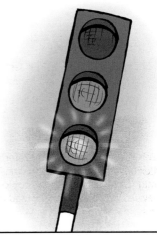

Planning revision timetables

Most students are guided to make complicated revision timetables linked to days of the week split into revision slots. You can offer a far simpler version. For each subject draw the following box.

- Each section represents, say, half an hour's revision
- Student colours in the section when half an hour is done
- All six sections need to be coloured in by the end of a set time (eg a week)

This gives students who prefer more flexibility a clear model to use. They might prefer to write the topics revised into the boxes instead of colouring them in.

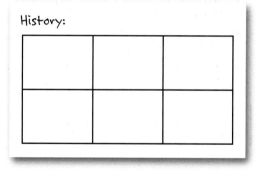

History:

Cut them off in their prime

A cardinal revision need is for students to practise writing to time. You have to be brutal in order for students to realise **the need for speed**. Try some of the following:

- A loud alarm clock – a particularly effective way to time students' work
- Give a time limit and then shout out each time a minute passes
- Pair students to time each other, so introducing a competitive element into the activity
- Use three or four students as 'time wardens'. Their job is to take in students' work the moment time is up

If it's a question of speeding up the mechanical task of writing, students can use a stop watch to see how long it takes to write, say, the first verse of their favourite pop song. They then try to knock five seconds off that time. Over a period of a week they periodically time themselves, aiming for increased speed without losing legibility.

You need to give students plenty of practice with timed tasks, or all your creative teaching will leak away as students fail to use examination time well.

**Challenge Your
Comfort Zones**

 **Starting
Out**

 **Asking the
Right Questions**

 **Active
Learning**

 **Making
Technology
Work for You**

 **Creative
Lesson Ideas**

 **Revision
Aids**

 **Building a
Sense of
Teamwork**

Building a Sense
of Teamwork

Pulling together

A creative learning environment is built upon good relationships among all the groups of individuals who make up a school's population. Working together allows all people in the education process to contribute to a positive and enjoyable learning experience.

This chapter should help you, as a creative teacher, to develop that sense of teamwork so crucial to a positive learning environment. The first part looks at working as a team with your students, the second suggests ways in which you can build a sense of teamwork into your interactions with your colleagues.

Working with the students

Use evaluation exercises to put the students at the heart of the creative process. Put the following questions to the students to feed back their ideas into your teaching.

'Which parts of the course did you enjoy and why?'

'Which parts of the course did you find difficult?'

'Are there ways of working that you feel would be good to use when this course is taught to next year's students?'

'Are there any activities you would like to try in future lessons?'

When you then use some of the student advice, it boosts their self-esteem and shows them that they are part of shaping the learning process.

Engaging students with assessment

Work with your students to develop peer marking and involve them in setting marking criteria. In this way you will lead them not only to understand work better, but also into making creative suggestions as to how to cover it. This also helps students develop problem-solving skills.

Try to use a simple framework at first:

Level 1 response = simple statement/partly correct
Level 2 response = developed statement/ mostly correct
Level 3 response = developed argument/totally correct

Encourage students to think in levels, not grades. You can swap levels for colours, again using the traffic light sequence where level one is red, level two amber and level three green.

Peer teaching

With careful resourcing and teacher-modelling of activities, peer teaching is a very effective way of generating teamwork, as well as giving students a different perspective on the learning process.

- Ask students to plan and deliver lessons, or parts of lessons, after showing them parts of the scheme of work
- Ask sixth form or Y11 students to teach a lower school lesson

This practice challenges and engages both 'teacher' and audience. It allows students to creatively deliver information to a target audience and can lead participants to a more sympathetic view of how difficult teaching a class can be.

Thinking about success

Three key questions

Encourage your students to think about success. Use three key questions to stimulate discussion and move them on to a new level of self-knowledge:

1. Why was your most successful piece of work a success?
Get the students to look at the idea of 'success' from different angles rather than just choosing work that earned top marks, eg they might consider work that they had to really think through to produce.

2. What skills do you need to succeed at this subject?
The second question will focus tightly on the specific skills needed to succeed within your subject. This will allow you to engage with the students and show them how you can all build the necessary skills and move towards success. Ground the outcomes in a display for all years to see.

Thinking about success

Three key questions

You can now help the students to step back and consider themselves as learners. Encourage them to review personality traits and interests that help them succeed as learners.

3. What is it about you that makes you a successful learner?
Common responses include: *'I am stroppy and like to argue'; 'I am determined'; 'I like to prove people wrong'* and *'I enjoy finding out about new things'*.

Use the responses to build an 'ideal student' display!

Using students' work

Using students' work to teach others is a clear sign that you value their efforts and see them as working in tandem with you. There are some easy ways to use students' work as teaching resources:

- Teach from display work
- Combine students' homeworks to make information packs
- Pull students' ideas on to mind maps and use those as core texts for the lesson
- Get students to create worksheets for other classes to use
- Ask students to put together booklets that you will use instead of textbooks
- Work with students to produce revision guides

Sharing and using ideas like these will enhance the learning process for both you and your students.

Tasks to build teamwork

How you set up work can also encourage a sense of student participation in the learning process. The following are useful tasks for teamwork-building:

- Ask students to recommend and rank
- Set students up to judge and evaluate
- Encourage students to combine, modify and rearrange work
- Get students to select and use

Resource banks

Equally, you can help students to work independently by setting **up resource banks and information points** in your room which they can visit freely to support their classroom tasks.

One useful set up is to have a corner of the room with display targeted to literacy and subject-specific advice. In the same corner have a table/trolley or shelf of useful items such as dictionaries, thesauruses and rough paper. Go there yourself to access dictionaries and get paper to make notes on. The students will begin to follow your lead, and the resource zone will become a shared office-like location.

Working creatively with colleagues

All teachers have plenty of ideas to share. But in the everyday business of teaching there is precious little time to swap activities. A key to creative teaching is to *make that time to share good practice*. You might have a standing agenda in department meetings for discussing good practice and ideas. But you can also share ideas through team-teaching, collectively planning a run of lessons, and by setting up effective systems for feeding back from professional development courses.

Working with support staff

You should aim to involve support staff in your lesson-planning activities. Teaching assistants and clerical support staff are invaluable sources of ideas and information. Some TA's may have far more experience of particular students in different learning contexts than you. They may well be able to suggest ways of working that have engaged a class in other subjects and could be worth trying in your lessons. Clerical staff may suggest a more effective way of presenting information, or may have useful anecdotal evidence from their own children's education.

Working with outside agencies

Look for resource opportunities as well as the more traditional approach of inviting talks and theatre groups. Aim to build links into the local community via local groups and businesses.

- Approach organisations like the Round Table for potential speakers and sponsors
- Contact professional organisations like accountancy firms who may have a high turnover of useful teaching props like coloured paper and pens
- Contact local voluntary organisations and charities to see what they might be able to offer as resources, speakers, or other contacts
- Use work experience links to ask for materials

Always follow up contacts and keep a list.

ASK BIG!
If you don't ask you don't get.

Forums for sharing good practice

There are many opportunities to develop forums for good practice.

- Standing agenda item on department and staff meetings
- Ideas pinboard in the staff room
- Good practice bulletin compiled by teacher suggestions to SMT
- The pub after school

Keep an archive of good ideas to build up and circulate as you develop your teaching career.

Peer observation

Peer observation is a powerful tool for sharing creative practice. Set some basic ground rules first to maximise impact:

- Set up a small peer team of between 3-5 colleagues
- Agree simple protocols regarding recording of observation and feedback
- Set specific observation focuses each time, eg lesson openings
- Look to set up cross-curricular peer teams to enrich the sharing of ideas

Peer observation is a non-threatening way of developing your creative skills as a teacher. (The Lesson Observation Pocketbook will support you in developing this type of observation.)

The **Lesson Observation Pocketbook** by Roy Watson-Davis published by Teachers' Pocketbooks, 2009

Moderating students' work

One of the benefits of moderating sessions is that you can see how colleagues have delivered the same content as you. At these meetings swap student workbooks to look for ideas you can use. Also, use the moderation session as a forum for swapping creative ideas about lesson delivery.

- Aim to look at one year group's work each half-term
- Use a manageable sample from your classes – two books from high performing students, two from the middle, and a couple of lower grade books

Feed the data from these sessions into making schemes of work more creative too.

The use of opposites

When you seek the advice of colleagues over how to deliver aspects of a lesson, it's worth sometimes going to the department as far removed from your own as possible for a fresh angle. So, if you teach a predominantly active subject like drama or PE, seek out mainly non-active subjects like ICT or geography. This has the added benefits of helping to set up cross-curricular activities and of encouraging inter-staff co-operation, a key motivator for creative teaching strategies.

Checklist

This half term have you:

Shared one of your ideas with a colleague? ❏
Asked for advice from a colleague in your department? ❏
Involved the TA in some aspect of your planning? ❏
Sought ideas from a non-subject-specialist colleague? ❏
Moderated student work for inspiration? ❏
Phoned or talked to an outside agency? ❏
Observed a colleague teach? ❏
Shared a laugh and a joke in the staffroom? ❏
Team-taught a lesson? ❏
Planned work with one or more colleagues? ❏
Praised or thanked a colleague for help? ❏
Chipped in an idea without being asked? ❏
Looked at resources with colleagues? ❏
Rewritten a lesson and shared it with your department? ❏
Changed a display? ❏

Bibliography

The Accelerated Learning Pocketbook by Brin Best
Published by Teachers' Pocketbooks, 2003

Because We Can Change the World: A Practical Guide to Building Co-Operative Classroom Communities by Mara Sapon-Shevin
Published by Alleyn and Bacon, 1999

Consulting Pupils: A Toolkit for Teachers by Macbeath, Demetriou, Rudduck and Myers
Published by Pearson, 2003

Creating Your Classroom Community by Lois Bridges
Published by Stenhouse, 1995

E-Learning in the 21st Century by D Garrison and T Anderson
Published by Routledge, 2003

Learning to Teach by Neville Bennet and Clive Carre
Published by Routledge, 1993

Taxonomy of Educational Objectives: The Classification of Educational Goals by Benjamin S. Bloom
Published by Longmans, 1969

www.thelearningkit.org.uk   www.alite.co.uk

Further reading on Active Learning: DfES 0434-2004 Pedagogy and Practice: Teaching and Learning in Secondary Schools, Unit 11: Active engagement techniques.

About the author

Roy Watson-Davis

Roy has been teaching History since 1992. From 2001-2010 he worked as an AST in south east London specialising in non-subject-specific teaching and learning, and behaviour management. He supported colleagues in schools in Special Measures or with Notice to Improve, as well as providing general staff development and mentoring. He has written three Teachers' Pocketbooks, *Creative Teaching*, *Form Tutor's* and *Lesson Observation*. Having escaped to the country, Roy is currently working as Head of History at Northgate High School in Suffolk.

Acknowledgements

I would like to thank colleagues past and present, especially Fred Valletta and Matt Brown at Blackfen School, Sidcup. Also my current head, Dave Hutton, for taking a bit of a punt on me. I find inspiration in many quarters and thanks also go to Simon Robinson and all at the Deep Purple Appreciation Society, the music of Motorhead, and my cats Buster and Mazey.

Order form

Your details

Name _____

Position _____

School _____

Address _____

_____

_____

Telephone _____

Fax _____

E-mail _____

VAT No. (EC only) _____

Your Order Ref _____

Please send me:

		No. copies
Creative Teaching	Pocketbook	
_____	Pocketbook	
_____	Pocketbook	
_____	Pocketbook	

Order by Post

Teachers' Pocketbooks
Laurel House, Station Approach
Alresford, Hants. SO24 9JH UK

Order by Phone, Fax or Internet
Telephone: +44 (0)1962 735573
Facsimile: +44 (0)1962 733637
Email: sales@teacherspocketbooks.co.uk
Web: www.teacherspocketbooks.co.uk

Customers in USA should contact:
2427 Bond Street, University Park, IL 60466
Tel: 866 620 6944   Facsimile: 708 534 7803
Email: mp.orders@ware-pak.com
~~~~~~~~~~~~~~~~~~~~ementpocketbooks.com